♡ **L O V E** children's books and comics
✿ **L I F E** comics and graphic novels
☻ **D E A T H** one-off art books and publications

You will find the name of the series on our website under each book title as well as on the back cover of each book by the barcode.

The publication of this translation has been made possible through the financial support of

MINISTRY OF CULTURE CZECH REPUBLIC

Savages, Lucie Lomová
First published in Great Britain in 2023 by Centrala Ltd.
35 Oriental Place apt 1
Brighton BN1 2LL

Copyright © Centrala Ltd., 2023
Copyright © Actes Sud – l'An 2, France, 2011
First published in France as Les Sauvages by Actes Sud – l'An 2 in 2011
Translation © Julia and Peter Sherwood
Editorial & Publishing Director: Michał Słomka
DTP: gabinet.co.uk

All rights reserved. No portion of this book may be reproduced, stored in a retrieval system, or transmitted in any form or by any means, mechanical, electronic, photocopying, recording, or otherwise, without written permission from the publisher.
A CIP record for this book is available from the British Library

Printed and bound in Poland

ISBN 978-1-912278-38-1

Order from www.centrala.org.uk

Lucie Lomová

SAVAGES

TRANSLATION Julia and Peter Sherwood

Brighton 2023

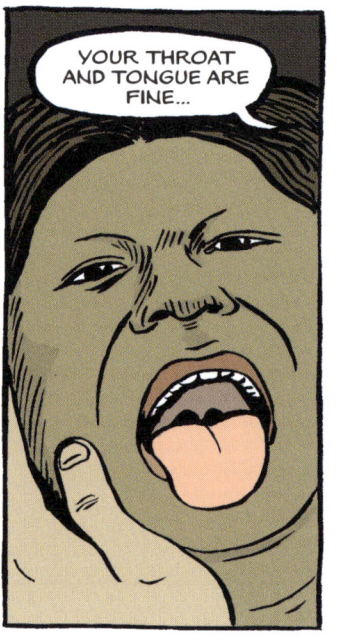

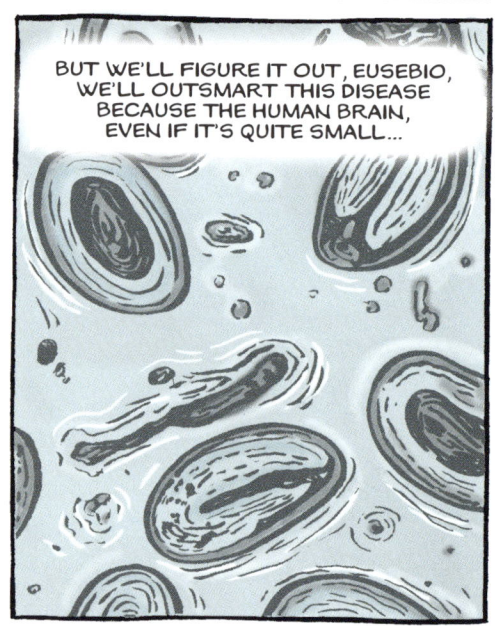

CHIEF ANTONIO!

ALBERTO, MY FRIEND!

ALBERTO, YOU'VE BEEN ON MY MIND DAY AND NIGHT. AND THEN I HEARD THAT YOUR BOAT IS HERE. SO WE'VE COME TO SEE YOU STRAIGHT AWAY.

THE LOCAL INDIANS ARE SICK. IT'S PROBABLY CONTAGIOUS. YOU SHOULD KEEP AWAY FROM THE SETTLEMENT.

IT'S TOO LATE FOR THAT. MY PEOPLE ARE ALSO SICK. WE'VE PITCHED CAMP WITH THE OTHERS.

CAN YOU MAKE US BETTER? YOU KNOW SO MUCH ABOUT INVISIBLE ANIMALS, YOU HAVE ALL KINDS OF MAGIC PILLS...

I'LL DO MY BEST, ANTONIO.

I'VE ASKED A FEW BOYS TO LIGHT BEACONS AND SUMMON THE CHAMACOCO FROM THE INTERIOR. WE'LL HOLD A BIG MEETING OF ELDERS TONIGHT.

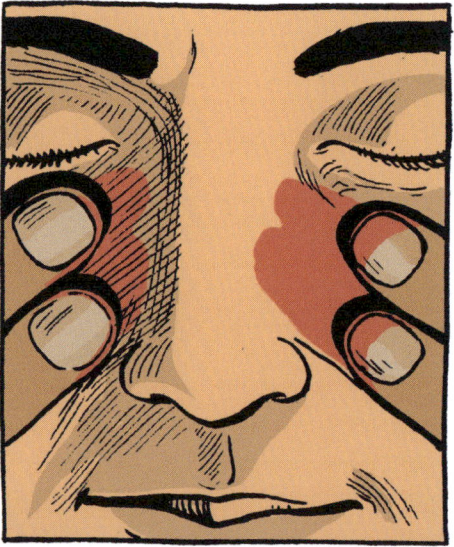

"COME ON, I CAN'T KEEP THE EDITOR WAITING."

"YOU WAIT OUTSIDE. I'LL BE BACK IN A MINUTE. AND DON'T GO ANYWHERE!"

* GIVE ME SOME MONEY FOR SAUSAGES, THEY MUST BE SO TASTY AND I'M STARVING...

** ...HE'S BACK ALREADY – AND ANGRY AGAIN)

I PICKED HIM UP AND TRIED TO FIND A PLACE TO THROW HIM TO THE GROUND.

BUT THERE WAS NO GRASS THERE, JUST STONES. SO I THREW HIM INTO THE RIVER SO HE WOULDN'T GET HURT.

BUT THEN MORE SHAMANS CAME RUNNING AND WANTED TO WRESTLE ME, ALL AT ONCE.

I FOUGHT BACK AS BEST I COULD. BUT THEN OTHERS CAME AND WANTED TO RIP MY BEAUTIFUL NEW SHIRT!

THEY GRABBED ME THE WAY ANTS GRAB A CENTIPEDE AND BROUGHT ME HERE.

I WAS WORRIED THAT ALBERTO WOULDN'T BE ABLE TO TRACK ME ON THE STONE PAVEMENT, SO I STARTED TO SING THE SAD SONG.

* GLORY! GLORY! GLORY!! REJOICE! GLORY! GLORY! GLORY! I REJOICE! I'VE DEFEATED THE EVIL SHAMANS AND MADE THEM FEED ME!

** THEY WERE MANY AND I WAS ALL ALONE!

*** MY GOOD FRIEND ALBERTO HAS FOUND ME AND IS REJOICING WITH ME! GLORY! GLORY! GLORY! I, VICTORIOUS CHERWUISH, REJOICE TOO!

* SLUT

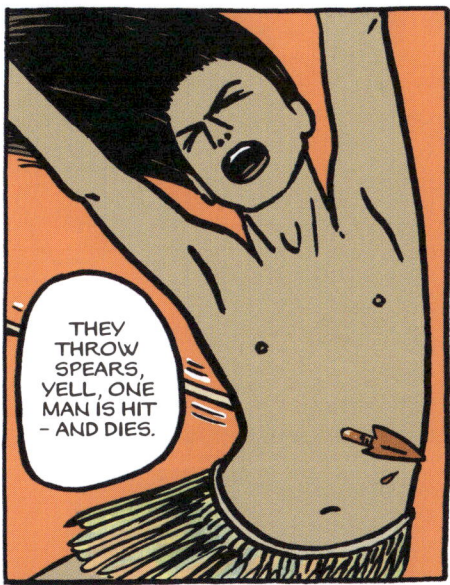

* JAROSLAV HAŠEK, AUTHOR OF THE GOOD SOLDIER ŠVEJK

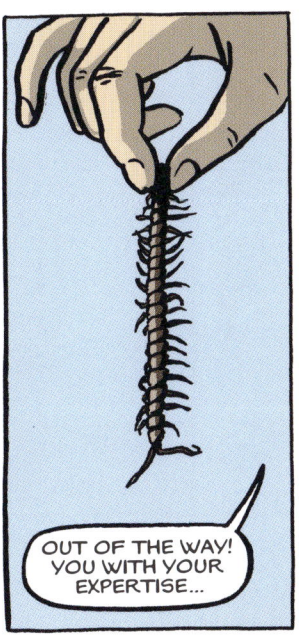

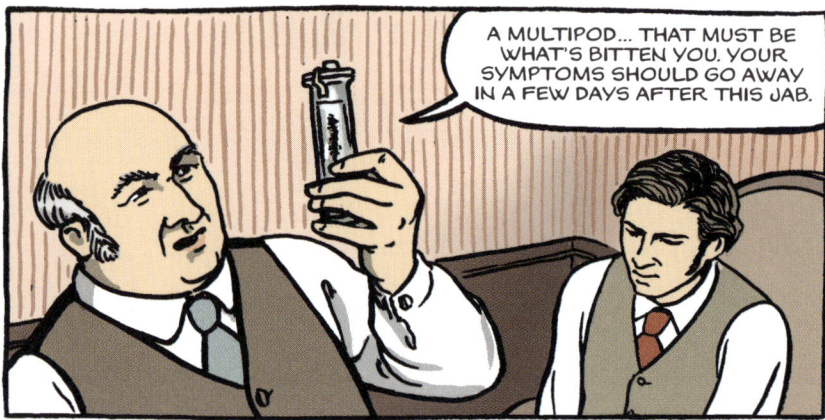

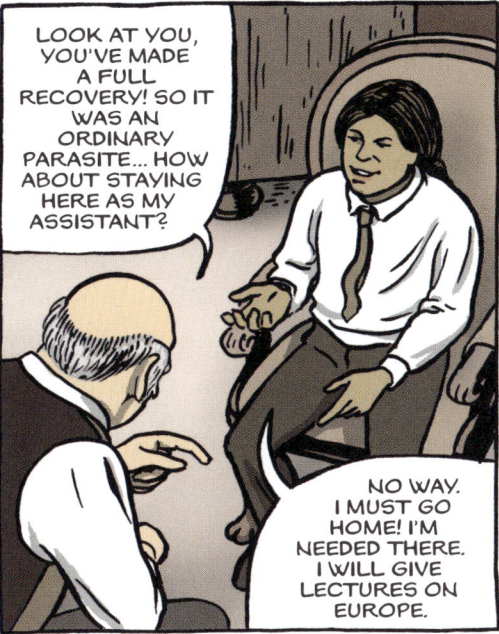

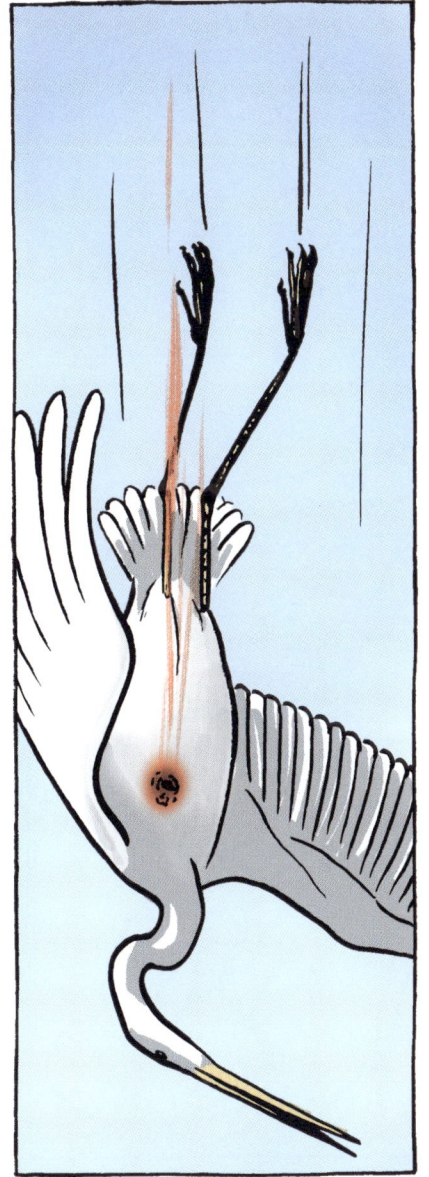

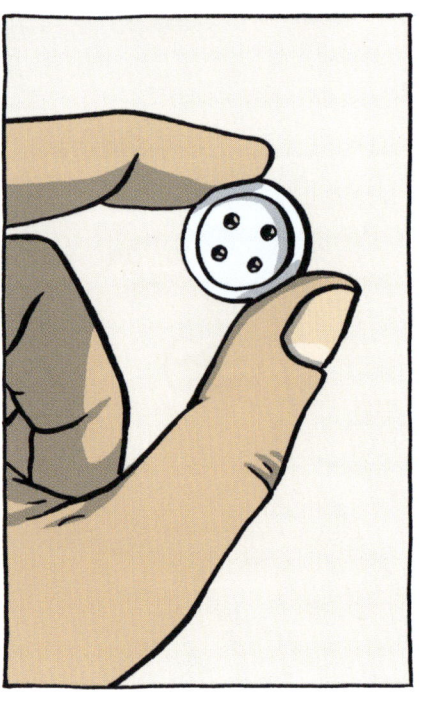

Cherwuish in Prague 1908 – 1909

Postscript

The story of Cherwuish is a true story. And it was in every respect as incredible, amusing and bittersweet as Lucie Lomová has drawn it. First published in instalments in the popular Czech journal *Pestrý týden* in 1943, it was written in his old age by the legendary explorer and collector of cacti A.V. Frič. In those days, as a protest against the German occupation of Czechoslovakia, he grew a full beard of the kind favoured by South American *barbudos*, and would not leave his house. During World War II writing became one of the few sources of his income. The adventures of a savage in the civilised world, written with grace, humour and empathy, gradually expanded into a great existential narrative – not just that of Cherwuish but equally of Frič's own personal story. The tale of a brave adventurer, a free spirit who sometimes acted impulsively, a dreamer and a brawler, an intrepid explorer of blank spots on the global map and in the human mind, endowed with a great gift for observation and also for asking good questions, an interpreter of truths experienced at first hand, a defender of the values of otherness.

The explorer, ethnographer, botanist, photographer, writer and unorthodox thinker Alberto (in Czech Vojtěch) Frič (1882-1944) came from a well-known patriotic family which left a significant mark on the political, cultural and scientific life of Czech society from the second half of the nineteenth century onwards. The stubborn youngest son, Frič was more interested in his cacti (still a botanical rarity in Europe at the time) than in most of the boring school subjects. While still a schoolboy, he accumulated one of the largest collection of exotic plants in Europe, becoming an internationally recognized expert. As he studied for his school leaving examination he failed to look after his greenhouses and one freezing night his entire collection succumbed to frost. In 1901, barely nineteen years old, he set out for Brazil to start a new collection, rather than going on to university. The year spent overseas proved to be a tough introduction to the school of life. He paddled down rivers from São Paulo in an Indian canoe all the way to the Mato Grosso, where he was almost mauled to death by a jaguar. By the time his wounds healed, Frič had decided to delve even further into the interior, and on his next expedition he was to find Indians untouched by civilisation.

Between 1903 and 1913 he undertook three exploratory trips through what is now Argentina, Bolivia, Brazil, Paraguay and Uruguay. He mapped the Pilcomayo river, carried out the first archaeological digs in *sambaqui* (prehistoric landfills), and came into contact with dozens of tribes from Pantanal and Chaca Boreal down to Patagonia. He stood out from other explorers by his humane attitude to the indigenous people, an understanding of their mentality, and a remarkable ability to communicate with them. He collected a vast quantity of sociological and ethnolinguistic material, recorded indigenous myths, gained insights into shamanistic medicine, acquired thousands of ethnographic objects for the world's museums, and made valuable contributions to every Americanist congress in the early twentieth century. At great personal cost and despite hurdles in the way of his research, he spoke out for the rights of the Indians and the preservation of their native culture. His uncompromising opposition to hypocrisy, lies and dilettantism in science, his outspoken manner and blistering journalistic style made him many enemies among influential scientists and politicians. He published scholarly articles in a variety of languages but is remembered mainly for his popularising features and stories aimed at the wider reading public, including children and young adults. The fact that he was self-taught – a handicap in the academic world – proved to be a great advantage to him as a writer. In America he made a living mostly by working as a journalist

Mr Indian, 1906 – 1908

A. V. Frič, photographed by V.J. Bufka around 1915

Cherwuish in a photograph taken in Domažlice, 1908-1909

reporting from the pampas and serving as a war correspondent.

Frič turned his South American experiences into works of fiction, written in his inimitable style. They include *Zákon pralesa* (1917, Law of the Jungle), *Mezi indiány* (1919, Among the Indians), *O kaktech a jejich narkotických účincích* (1924, On Cacti and Their Narcotic Effects), *Strýček indián* (1936, Mr Indian), *Indiáni Jižní Ameriky* (1942, The Indians of South America), *Dlouhý lovec* (1943 The Long Hunter), *Hadí ostrov* (1946, Serpent Island) and *Čerwuiš* (first edition in book form 1995, Cherwuish).

After the founding of Czechoslovakia he represented the new state on a diplomatic mission to Argentina and Uruguay (1919-1920), contributing significantly to the promotion of his native country overseas. He devoted his entire life to championing South America in the Czech Lands, regarding it as his sacred duty to publish and inform the public and prospective travellers and immigrants about his experiences and the opportunities that awaited them on the far side of the Atlantic. In the 1920s practically every Czech who contemplated settling in Argentina sought Frič's advice, either in person or in writing.

In 1923 he went on a botanical expedition to Mexico and his report from the journey and the huge number of unique finds spurred an unprecedented interest in cacti throughout Europe. As a result of his bad experience with commercial plant collectors he tried to conceal the location of cactus habitats and details of his travel routes. Nevertheless, we know that in 1927 he travelled all the way from Patagonia to Tucuman and back to Buenos Aires, via Santiago, the Chaco, Corrientes and the Andes, collecting an impressive array of seeds and live cacti, bromeliads and orchids on the way. In 1928-1929 he made his last journey, from Buenos Aires to the mountain ranges in the northwest on the borders with Argentina, Chile and Bolivia, which yielded significant botanical discoveries (such as *Rebulobivia einsteinii*) that exceeded all his expectations and caused a sensation among experts. In the 1930s and 1940s, back in the Czech Lands, he focused on cultivating plants and genetics, creating unique new plant species by grafting, hybridizing and irradiating. When severe frost at the beginning of World War II destroyed his Prague cactus collection, one of the largest in the world, he turned his attention to the experimental cultivation of useful plants. He died of tetanus in December 1944 after scratching himself on a rusty nail while cleaning out a rabbit hutch.

Although Frič's autobiographical adventure stories had a huge impact on several generations of Czech adolescents, these days fathers and grandfathers find it hard to get their offspring interested in his writing. And although he continues to enjoy an unequalled guru status among Czech cacti growers, his name is barely known abroad because he refused to switch to the new classification of cacti adopted internationally in the 1930s. His work is rarely cited by anthropologists (little of his writing has been translated into other languages) and he continues to suffer from a reputation as a wayward adventurer, bolstered by his jealous contemporaries in museum circles. His life has been covered by the dust-laden curtain of time.

However, a hundred years after the end of Cherwuish's story another story began. Two young Czechs with a camera set out for America in search for the Chamacoco village where Cherwuish's European adventure once began. They had no trouble finding it, as Frič provided quite an accurate description of it in his memoirs. They even found some individuals who remembered Cherwuish and said that he lived until the 1970s and died childless. He became known as an expert on the civilised world, his reputation increasing steadily from the moment the first airplane flew over the Chaco. However, no one remembered Frič. Not even the ancient indigenous woman who bore his surname. There is no mention of her in Frič's manuscripts or diaries: all that remains is the story of a sweet love affair with an Indian girl Lorai – Black Duck. He abandoned her in 1905 to attend an Americanist Congress and later regretted having missed out on the love of his life. Baby Herminia grew up without a father (and soon also without a mother), in the care of a friend of Alberto's, a local hunter. In her youth she was famed for her beauty, and her pale skin and light hair astonished anthropologists, who started visiting the Chamacoco in increasing numbers, eager to record their rapidly vanishing civilisation. In 2000, when the Czech film maker duo found Herminia, by then a frail grandmother, she asked them to tell the Czech relatives whom she had never known that she was still waiting for them.

And lo and behold, her wishes were conveyed to Frič's Czech descendants (he married in middle age and fathered one child, a son, in 1922). It was Frič's grandson Pavel and his wife Yvonna who plucked up the courage to seek

A. V. Frič with an orchid, 1943; photo by his son Ivan

Doña Herminia Ferreira Frič, with her relatives, 2008

out their remarkable aunt and her relatives in South America – the five generations of Herminia's extended family comprise some 200 people.

The homeland of the Chamacoco has undergone tremendous change over the past hundred years. Their forests have been cleared, the egrets killed, their traditions and superstitions wiped out. They are no longer allowed to roam the land freely, hunt for wild animals and crocodiles, gather fruit, catch fish, build fires and pitch camp wherever they please. Their lost paradise has been parcelled out and corralled in by the fences of the ranchers. But it still remains their beloved Gran Chaco, known among white people as "green hell" – one of the least hospitable parts of the world, and the Indians continue to be proud of their heritage. Some add that they are also a bit *checo* (Czech), demonstrating a typically Czech sense of humour. Frič's ancestors in the Czech Republic and Paraguay, who have found each other half a century after his death, have set up an NGO called *Checomacoco*.

The Czechs are trying to support the former nomads who have been forced to settle down, so that they can enjoy the same kind of life as the rest of the population in the impoverished Paraguayan countryside who end up in the capital's slums but instead can find work locally. So that their children have access to education and feel able to take their future into their own hands. So that they are motivated to support their village which their parents have named, for their sake, Puerto Esperanza. The Czech relatives have raised funds for a number of projects relating to agriculture, education, health and water supply. Some 400 cattle graze in the "Czech corral" outside the village, a simple sprinkler system irrigates their fields, the local school has been fitted with a new roof, the local health centre supplied with medicines, the fishermen have received two freezers for storing their catch, and local women two sewing machines. Several children are pursuing higher education.

A. F. Frič's last book, *Indiáni Jižní Ameriky* (The Indians of South America, published by Novina in 1943) bears a melancholy dedication to "his friends who, obedient to honour and their law, have died out". Not long after he wrote this, his own bow, as the Indians say, broke, releasing his soul into the realm of shadows, to hunt for the souls of ostriches and prepare a feast for the souls of his former hosts. If the souls of the dead really end up in the happy hunting grounds, he will have encountered the soul of his daughter Herminia, who would have informed him how wrong he was. His Chamacoco are alive and well, and their children born in recent years often bear Czech names.

Herminia died in spring 2009, aged 104. As a young girl, during hot tropical nights, she was likely to have heard Cherwuish's plaintive songs, reminiscing about his lecture tour around snow-covered Bohemia. And although the lyrics of Cherwuish's songs in this book are by Lucie, they appear here in the language of the Chamacoco, translated into her native tongue by Frič's great-great-grandaughter Hadasa, a student of environmental sciences. She typed them up on her laptop and emailed them to Prague, thus continuing this magnificent story whose origins go back some hundred years to the Northern Chaco.

Yvonna Fričová

www.checomacoco.cz

ACKNOWLEDGEMENTS

My heartfelt thanks go to Yvonna and Pavel Frič for so generously providing me with invaluable information and advice; the French publisher Thierry Groensteen for his unwavering support and valuable comments; the Czech publisher Joachim Dvořák and to my dear friend and publisher Michał Słomka; Jolana Součková, who first drew my attention to Cherwuish's story many years ago; Andrea Fajkusová and Lilian Hadasa Baez Martinez for the translation of the lyrics into the Chamacoco language; Irena Dousková for her useful advice; Pili Munoz and Brigitte Macias from the Maison des Auteurs for their kindness, care and assistance, as well as the staff of Atelierhaus Salzamt in Linz and my fellow residents for their helpfulness and friendship; Isabelle Rabillon, Philippe Leduc and Marc-Antoine Matthieu for their help, insightful comments and advice. I would also like to thank Ina Pouant of the Institute Français in Prague, Martin Čihák, my dear sister Ivana Lomová, my cousins Petr Lom and Anna Lom-Štefaník; and, last but not least, my wonderful children Vašek and Běta Suchan, who have traversed the world in this story with me with patience and interest. I am also grateful to the Ministry of Culture of the Czech Republic for financial support towards the publication of this book.

Lucie Lomová